WHAT ABOUT LOVE?

QUOTES TO DEEPEN YOUR UNDERSTANDING OF LOVE

ERIC CHIFUNDA

The EC Publishing LLC books may be ordered
through booksellers or by contacting:

EC Publishing LLC
116 South Magnolia Ave.
Suite 3, Unit F
Ocala, FL 34471, USA
Direct Line: +1 (352) 644-6538
Fax: +1 (800) 483-1813
http://www.ecpublishingllc.com/

Ordering Information:
Quantity sales. Special discounts are available on quantity purchases by corporations, associations, and others. For details, contact the publisher at the address above.

Printed in the United States of America

OTHER BOOKS BY ERIC CHIFUNDA

The Quest for God's Love (Pinnacle Book Achievement Award Winner)

Selected Inspirational Quotes (Pinnacle Book Achievement Award Winner)

Potent Quotes for Soul

Contents

Introduction

Life aims to provide us with opportunities in many different ways and guises, sometimes as challenges, that can help soften our rough edges so that we can become polished progressively in all aspects of our lives. Our highest goal, consciously or unconsciously, is to become the best version of ourselves and, more importantly, to realize the highest love innate in all of us. It's worth noting that our capacity for love varies from person to person, predicated on our attitude and level of consciousness, the degree to which our heart is open to give and receive love. The higher our consciousness, the greater our capacity for love. Awakening to love within and all around us can be facilitated by various practices, if done consistently, that are designed to uplift, such as meditation, prayer, HU chant (an ancient name for God), or whatever other uplifting ways taught in each individual's respective spiritual path.

Love flows from God to our hearts, which we then share with others through our loving actions. This love is at the core of who we are as Souls. If we would give love unconditionally, without strings attached, we would open others' hearts, which would help make this world a better place for ourselves and others.

Therefore, our task is to take advantage of opportunities that enable us to continually grow in our capacity for more love. With increased capacity for love comes a heightened sense of well-being, inner peace, and freedom. For this love to be of real value to us, we must not hoard it: We must share it with others in our day-to-day lives. This can be done in various ways, such as being kind, gentle to the weak, and being there for others in their hour of need. It helps to remember that it is by giving love that we receive love and life's blessings. With its attendant blessings, such unconditional love can enrich our lives beyond measure.

Acknowledgements

My profound heartfelt gratitude goes to Harold Klemp, my spiritual mentor, friend, and teacher, for his unfailing support and guidance on my spiritual journey.

ALL QUOTES ARE FROM
ERIC CHIFUNDA'S WRITINGS

Chapter 1

LOVE

LOVE

Love is an abstract concept, but it is one with practical significance. Therefore, action is required to express it. However, a wrong act can limit and distort the flow of love. To express love correctly, align your actions with the wishes of your loving heart. Balance these with humility and patience. Take it slow, at love's pace, so your heart agrees with your actions. Rushing things or even moving too slowly may ruin the process. Most importantly, firstly, listen to your heart and pay attention to the other person's needs; your heart will lead you to engage in the right action and move at the right pace. This way, you will be able to act appropriately to express love. Thus making love a practical reality in your day-to-day life.

THE INVISIBLE FORCE
CALLED LOVE

Within each person's inner sanctum is love, hidden in unknown places you never think to look as it awaits your discovery. It behooves you to remember that nothing exists without love at its epicenter, concealed from profane minds and closed hearts. Therefore, your task is to purify your heart to discover the latent love in those hidden places within you. Once awakened to this profound love, your heart expands, uplifting your consciousness. This invisible divine force called love revitalizes your life and enhances your well-being.

THE FORCE OF LOVE

Whenever your actions move life forward positively, the force behind it is always that of love, though it is not always recognized and understood as such. This is so because it comes under different guises depending on the prevailing circumstances. So, any actions done with and motivated by love improve inner and outer conditions. By the conditions you find yourself in today, you shall know the nature of the seeds you sowed yesterday. The force of love behind your actions will always yield good fruit, if not now, then later.

THE EXPANSIVE NATURE OF LOVE

Love, in its true form, always expands life, making it more abundant. Love is an essential part of our survival and existence. It's the only element that, when shared selflessly, increases in proportion and value. It diminishes in its outflow when we hoard it until it eventually diminishes and dies. Why? It is a universal force that operates best in an environment of freedom whereby it freely flows in from its inexhaustible God source and out through all of us, its channels, into the universe. Therefore, keeping it and restricting it to oneself in a personal realm runs counter to its expansive nature. Its higher purpose is for us to share with others. Its value, therefore, lies in our ability to give it out to the universe where it belongs, where it can make a change for the better- for the greater good.

THE FIRST TASK OF LOVE

How do you love others such that true love prevails? You must start by understanding the fundamental requirement of love: to learn how to listen to others. In learning to listen, you tune in to the needs of the people you interact with and those you serve and love, such as friends, family, coworkers, clients, and even strangers. Therefore, love's first task is to listen. If someone is hurt, stop and listen to their pain as needed and as you are able. In listening, you understand their needs and how best to serve them.

THE INNER CORE OF YOU

In the inner recesses of your physical temple exists the core of you—The Soul that has the power to love. Soul is the real you outside the superficiality of Its outer physical and psychic garments. It is Soul that lends life to the lower, outer physical clothing that It needs to express Itself on this physical plane of existence visible to the human eye. Through this external, physical point of contact, Soul can express Its love to those open and receptive to It. And your primary duty is to know yourself and discover your inner core—you as Soul.

ACTING WITH LOVE

To act with love, learn to follow your heart. How do you know you are following your heart so you can act with love? How do you determine whom to give love to? How do you figure out the amount of love you should give to someone? Asking a specific and clear question can hint at an insightful answer, leading to the right choices and, consequently, the right actions. It behooves you to listen to your heart and follow its promptings. Instinct, that inner heart impulse, can guide your loving actions without overanalyzing or intellectualizing. Too much mental analysis can cause confusion in the matters of heart-love that arise from a place beyond the mind realm.

In human relations, it helps to step back and let love flow without imposing it on another. Love will slip away if you try to possess another and be excessively controlling. So learn to step back and let love find its natural flow through your loving actions.

GIVING LOVE

Are you giving love out of a misguided feeling of pity for another? Are you doing it out of fear of being judged? Are you doing it out of guilt? Are you doing it out of superiority or a perceived sense of obligation? These basic yet essential questions may help elucidate, facilitate, and guide your decision-making about whether the love you are giving to another is appropriate, unconditional, and well-intentioned.

GIVING LOVE SELFLESSLY

Giving love selflessly makes life a little more forgiving for others, and in turn, the favorable conditions of like nature will come your way at an appropriate time. Even though, at times, what you give may require sacrifice, take comfort knowing that nothing is ever lost. Acts of sacrifice for another in need always lead to higher love not realized before. Life has a way of repaying people generously commensurate to their loving actions.

THE BEST WAY TO SAY 'I LOVE YOU'

Simple acts of love can create trust between people and foster love within their hearts in a way that exaggerated gestures may not. Sharing love honestly is the best way to say I love you. Do it through actions, not just words alone. If not backed up by requisite actions, words are just empty promises. Therefore, the best way to say "I love you" is to demonstrate it through your loving actions. Walk the walk!

APPROPRIATELY MAKING LOVE A HEALTHY REALITY

How do you appropriately make love a healthy reality, not something you promise or discuss? If you learn to love without conditions, love will blossom, thus becoming a healthy reality. Avoid giving it to satisfy your ego, out of fear, or out of the need to appease someone without basis in truth. Be sincere, truthful, and courageous, and the love you give will become a healthy reality in your life. With love like this, your life can't help but expand and become enriched. To make love a healthy reality, the right action that serves as a carrier for love is needed, for it is in doing that you make love a reality, not something you talk about, but indeed something you live.

LOVE IN SMALL DEEDS

Love sometimes shows itself in small things. The problem is that these minor, commonplace deeds often go unnoticed. Thus, you must learn to be more aware of little acts of love. Be grateful for little deeds, the small gestures of love first. That is the vital starting point in learning to recognize love, which can lead to a greater and deeper appreciation for life. With great appreciation for life, your love capacity expands as love becomes your reward. Your heart will be increasingly open to giving and receiving love in greater measure.

CONNECTING SOUL TO SOUL THROUGH LOVE

Love is a gift that genuinely connects Soul to Soul more profoundly when given from the heart. Sincerity in love creates healthier and more profound relationships between people, for it is truly love that bonds us all together. Ensure that the love you share with others is unconditional. This helps establish a loving connection with others, a Soul-to-soul connection. The feeling of love can permeate your entire being, rippling through your body, mind, and Soul.

LOVE, THE CATALYST FOR POSITIVE CHANGE

To make the world move forward to a higher level in which there's increased peace and order, the ingredient of love must play a vital role as an invisible prime mover. That is why every advancement brings dividends of positive outcomes in whatever area of human endeavor if love is the underlying guiding force. So, if you want to bring positive change in your life and society, ensure you do it with love and for love only—and that it is unconditional.

THE AUTHENTICITY OF LOVE

Even though the outer appearance can sometimes reflect what's on the inside, it is always helpful to look beyond. Steeped in materiality, many deceive others and give love with strings attached. Real love is not always obvious because we live in a world of illusion and deception, which tends to throw wool over our eyes. So, always look beyond the outer appearance to better understand the authenticity of the love given to you.

RISING TO NEW HEIGHTS THROUGH LOVE

Keep in mind that only unconditional love has the power to cause a shift in the ether, so the new ground breaks, and the world is subsequently lifted to new heights ever so slightly. Through your loving actions, large or small, your role in the world is to leave it in a better state than the one you found. Small, selfless acts serve as building blocks to improve conditions for self and others, continually raising life to new heights.

LOVE WITHOUT STRINGS ATTACHED

When love is allowed to flow freely, it touches those for whom it is intended and bestows upon them all things positive. Love uplifts. It opens the hearts of others. It nourishes, lifts, and honors those who are receptive to it. It has the power to heal a broken heart. Love can only be freely allowed to flow when the giver gives it unconditionally, without strings attached.

ACTIONS DRIVEN BY LOVE

Through actions driven by love, you get transformed into loving individuals. We can make love a way of life by learning how to open our hearts and by using ethical conduct. One cannot do it by merely talking about it. Talk is cheap; demonstrate love through loving actions to make it a living reality. Don't place conditions upon whomever you give it to; otherwise, it will cause an unpleasant reaction, breaking up good relationships and straining the love connection among those you love. Strive to continually engage in fair, uplifting, and truthful actions driven by love.

A LOVING ATTITUDE

It takes a loving attitude in which you put yourself in the other person's shoes to better understand their needs, without being judgmental, to give love properly. Therefore, how you give love can be influenced by your attitude. With the right attitude, you can easily give love to others when the need arises or when you want to please another to make them feel appreciated, given attention, and acknowledged. Without the right attitude, your expression of love will be misdirected and even stymied. Change your attitude, and you change how you love others. A loving attitude is a game-changer in all you do.

GIVING LOVE UNCONDITIONALLY

When you recognize and feel pure love in your heart, your consciousness begins to expand; this indicates an opening of your heart center to God's love, which you can pass on to others if given unconditionally. It helps to remember that conditional love limits the flow of love because of the attendant strings attached and a self-serving attitude. Strings attached are a limiting factor in sharing the love that opens others' hearts. So it behooves you to give love unconditionally and selflessly so more love can flow and deepen your connection with those you love.

LOVE IN YOUR HEART

When you place your attention on someone, and they evoke warm feelings of love, there's inner harmony between you both, irrespective of distance. Nurture this feeling, this inner link, this alliance, because it indicates mutual love in your hearts, uplifting one another to new heights and infusing you with a more profound sense of well-being. This pure, warm love soothes the hearts of those with whom it is shared and whose hearts are open.

WAYS THAT EXPRESS LOVE

What are some of the ways that best express love? ; Actions that are done without regard to whether you get recognized or not.; Actions performed without the need to seek attention; Actions executed without the need for praise; Actions performed with humility; Positive actions that lift another Soul in their hour of need without expecting anything in return; Actions that help open another person's heart to more love. ; Actions that one does well and to completion; Actions that honor another's divinity: Actions that help lift another Soul on their journey home to God. Actions that bring reassurance and solace to a troubled Soul : Actions that propel another to new heights in whatever their area of endeavor; Actions that empower another: Actions that bring joy to another. : Actions that instill hope and confidence that help heal a broken heart. : Actions that inspire others to live a better life ;

ACTING FROM A PLACE OF LOVE

We unwittingly block love by being judgmental of others; this makes it difficult to love the person you are judging. Being highly critical and resentful of another stops love from flowing toward that person. Condemning another for their mistakes will shut the love flow toward the person. Love may still be in motion, but not in the intended direction. It may flow in the wrong direction and not achieve its desired objective. To give love correctly, do it such that it adds value to the other person's life. By acting from a place of love selflessly, you may help fulfill others' needs, rendering their life and, in turn, yours a little more forgiving. Henceforth, life expands and is enriched for all concerned.

LOVING WITHOUT EXPECTATION OF ANYTHING IN RETURN

If you can give without expecting anything in return, without seeking praise, in whatever way and form, then you are giving unconditional love. This type of love enables one to grow and reach the highest peaks of one's heart, which yields a heightened sense of well-being. Perhaps one can look to God in that He gives all love without the expectation of giving it back. Similar to how the Sun provides us with its light without expecting us to give anything back. Practice such love as much as you can, and your life shall be elevated gradually beyond measure. For you are loving as God loves within the limits of your consciousness.

THE PASSAGE OF LOVE THROUGH YOU

To let love flow unobstructed, learn to step back and avoid undue attachment to the fruits of your actions, seek no recognition, and surrender to the moment and to God within. Doing so will steer you away from your inadvertent personal interference in the love flow. This attitude will enable you to work with the Divine Spirit to facilitate the passage of love through you as its clear channel to the world.

AN EXPANDED LOVE CAPACITY

Our experience and understanding of love change as we grow in our consciousness. Our understanding of God deepens as our consciousness expands; thus, our capacity for love expands. With increased love capacity, our life expands as we can handle more and touch, serve, and lift more Souls as we act from a place of expanded love capacity. Each new higher level we attain brings with it gifts of wisdom, inner strength, love, joy, and freedom. It behooves us to seek to expand our consciousness, and our life will be transformed, and our destiny positively altered, realigned, and recalibrated in a new and better direction.

Chapter 2

EXPANDING THE CAPACITY FOR LOVE

MAXIMIZING YOUR CAPACITY FOR LOVE

Each person has a God-given mission, whether one knows it or not. Discovering and fulfilling our mission and our life purpose is what we are here to do: to learn the ins and outs of life to survive in this world. We survive and truly awaken our consciousness to a level where we understand our role in life, our higher mission, and how to fulfill it. By fulfilling our mission, we fulfill God's dream for us. Thus, life should not be lived as a race in which you compete with others but as one in which you measure your pace and success based on what you were yesterday to better yourself today. Therefore, it helps to look at life as an individual journey with a mission to maximize our capacity for love. An expanded capacity for love aligns us with God's will. In an expanded state of awareness, our lives transform for the better.

ACCESSING HIGHER CONSCIOUSNESS THROUGH LOVE

Love is the key that enables one to access one's higher consciousness—not love in the general, social sense, but divine love. How is divine love different from human love? Divine love is the type of love that opens one's heart to God; it brings one closer to God because it is of godly properties. It is commonly known as the Holy Spirit in Christianity, called by other names in other paths. It comprises two aspects; these twin pillars are the Sound and Light of God. It is the voice of God heard in many different forms (verbal and nonverbal) and can be seen as light (blue light, yellow light, white light via your inner vision). Together, the Light and Sound are divine love, the spirit of God in action. Through such divine love, one can access one's higher consciousness. The expansion of consciousness can be attained by practicing or singing a HU song. HU is an ancient name for God that doesn't belong to any religion. Anyone can practice it and reap the rewards of practicing it. One's consciousness, awareness, and creativity expand if done with love and consistency.

A DEEPER CONNECTION WITH LIFE AND GOD

One with an expanded level of consciousness has a deeper understanding and connection with the spirit of God and tends to be more unconditionally loving. Unconditional love is a prerequisite to establishing a stronger relationship with life and God. Unconditional love is the connecting link between you as Soul, life, and God. Thus, coming from this vantage point and keeping your heart open creates a common thread that deeply links you to life and God.

EXPERIENCING LOVE IN ITS MANY FORMS

By raising your consciousness, you increase your capacity to see and feel the presence of love in all living forms. This is so because your inner spiritual faculties of sight and hearing become more acute, thus rendering you more perceptive and far-seeing. Problems become easier to solve, you feel more contented, and you attain a more positive outlook. So, it is helpful to raise your awareness to enable you to actively partake in love in its many subtle forms. Remember that everything God creates has love in it, even though you may not always see it. What you see is based on the level of consciousness from which you operate. The higher the consciousness, the more you can see and experience love in many forms.

A NEW PATHWAY

In Its inherent infinite intelligence, the Divine Spirit has bestowed upon you the gift of love and will prompt you on how best to distribute it. All you have to do is surrender to It and follow Its ways. Once you follow It, a new pathway will be paved—a path to where God wants you to share more of your gifts of love and lift others through your loving actions.

The attitude of surrendering to God plays a key role in enabling you to let go of old, outmoded ways and embark on a new pathway as you continue on your quest for God. Without surrender, you may resist getting on a new path that God places before you to start your new cycle of spiritual unfoldment. Surrender allows you to engage the life force, the essence of God, more actively. So, it directly impacts your life as it becomes an active, helpful part of your daily experiences.

PURIFICATION OF THE HEART

In the human state, humans exist in a continual survival mode for the human self. We are torn asunder within our inner consciousness, pulled up and down, buffeted left and right. Pulled up by the natural upward pull of the Divine Spirit as it flows back to its divine source and pulled down by the materiality of life. Our inner state becomes a constant battleground until one day, through long, arduous life experiences and the right spiritual training in our own respective path, and if practiced consistently and diligently, we learn how to lean upon the divine power for our guidance and survival. This takes purification of the heart, the upliftment of our consciousness, and the sacrifice of our human self for a higher, spiritual Self.

Travails, tribulations, misfortunes, and pains become the purifying agents to break up the dross, cut through the layers of insulation that block the light of God from reaching us to light up our inner worlds so we can awaken, and see the light of God and hear the voice of God more clearly. Love is the inner divine force facilitating this transformation and transmutation of our inner being—our inner consciousness. With the breaking up of the inner constraints that bind us to this outer material, psychic world, our hearts are rendered pure and free, allowing us to come into alignment with the essence of God.

SPIRITUAL AWAKENING

The expansion of your spiritual consciousness enables you to view life from a higher perspective, thus seeing things a little more clearly, which can lead to a positive change in your day-to-day life. With clearer sight, fear diminishes, your life expands, and you can extend love to more people and other living things. This is so because spiritual awakening opens your inner eyes and ears to see and hear the gift of love around you more clearly. This clarity of sight and increased capacity for love, born out of spiritual awakening, will enable you to see beyond the illusion of life. Such is a vital benefit of spiritual awakening.

LETTING GO AND SURRENDERING INTO GOD'S HANDS

What happens when you let go and surrender your undue attachments to God? How can you effectively surrender? Why is surrender vital in one's spiritual life? The initial step to surrender could be as basic as recognizing that material things are of impermanent value. Thus, don't place undue dependency on them. Doing so can create fear in you. Place your trust and reliance on the indestructible Divine Spirit. Surrender gradually leads to a life of freedom from the entrapments of this material world. When you surrender all into the hands of God, you gain what you need spiritually. And ultimately, you ascend to a higher version of yourself with love as your awakened inner guiding principle. As you surrender your life into God's hands, He works more directly through you to support and guide you according to His will. The challenge is gaining courage and mustering up enough self-discipline to follow through with your actions in a way consistent with God's guidance.

BECOMING A BETTER VERSION OF YOURSELF

Love makes you a better human being when embraced and expressed daily in whatever way possible. It transforms you into a better person who treats others fairly, respectfully, without malice, and without judging others. When love is allowed as an expression of your actions, your life expands. It becomes transformed, lifting you to become a better version of yourself.

AWAKENING FROM A SPIRITUAL SLUMBER

What happens when you gain entry into the inner core of your heart, wherein the hidden treasures of God's love lay? Your life undergoes a transformation in which your view of life expands. The curtain of illusion you have known as reality is relative and gets pulled away. You awaken from spiritual slumber and glimpse the unseen inner God world. A glimpse into this inner heaven world brings with it a heightened feeling of joy and love, and in turn, you lose the fear of death, for you now see a higher life beyond the temporary outer world of appearances. Awakening to this higher inner world likewise awakens and increases your capacity for love.

THE RIPPLING EFFECT OF LOVE

Love is the force of life that moves the world in a specific direction and order and always toward a better place, despite cycles of destruction and rebuilding of life locally and globally as our unique personal and collective global journeys trudge along. Human activity impacts the direction and conditions of life. Whatever we put into life will reflect today's prevailing conditions, for worse or better. It is helpful to remember that personal and global activities guided by love always build life, and without love, the reverse results in the destruction of life. We live in an impermanent world that inevitably undergoes its assigned natural cycle of birth, growth, and death as a necessary process to move forward at its appropriate time. At a personal level, love for others touches our hearts and extends beyond our immediate outer circles of friends and family with whom we are more familiar. With unconditional love transcending time and space, its effects will ripple out to all whose hearts are open and receptive to it.

MORE ROOM TO GROW

Our imperfections afford us a chance to continue to learn and grow. Since we cannot be God, the eternal, our learning process will continue as long as we are here on earth and beyond. There's always a reason for our sojourn here on earth. If there weren't a reason, we wouldn't be here. There are always new lessons to learn and more room to grow in our capacity for more love. It helps to remember that each person's degree of love and life lessons to learn are different. While your mission may ask you to take charge, the mission of another may be to step back and play a silent and supportive role. Hence, judge not another whose life and lessons differ from yours.

POLISHING YOUR ROUGH EDGES

As you keep moving forward, you will find life and your experiences more rewarding, making life more joyful. This does not mean there may not be pain, losses, or challenges in your life. There will be, as it is through such harsh experiences, that our rough edges get smoothed out to reveal our authentic, polished, loving selves. Despite the unpleasant things that may happen, our expanded consciousness will engender an increased capacity to understand and make difficult times easier to bear. The expanded understanding enables us to become more responsible, less judgmental, less critical, compassionate, and more loving.

THE DEEPENING OF LOVE

When there's mutual trust between two people that love each other, love deepens. This deepening of love creates a new pathway, leading to deeper love in one's heart and in areas of the heart not known before. No one can ever reach a point where they realize the ultimate fullness of love. It is endless; therefore, its growth in human hearts has no end. It will continually manifest itself in different ways to take relationships progressively to a higher level. Stay open to new ways love may appear to deepen and enrich your life.

SHARPENING YOUR ABILITY TO RECOGNIZE LOVE

There are many ways love comes to people that they may not recognize. How do you improve your ability to recognize love in disguise when it comes your way? You can strengthen your ability to recognize love by learning and diligently practicing spiritual exercises, meditation, prayer, or the HU chant. Expanding your consciousness increases your ability to see life around you and within you with increased clarity. With increased clarity in what you see, you will begin to recognize love in its many different forms and guises. It is always love in you that enables you to feel and see love in others.

FULFILLING YOUR LIFE

The awakening of consciousness increases the capacity for love and the ability to understand the vital role of God's invisible presence in your life. You better understand the significance of aligning your actions with God's guidance. You realize that without consciously engaging with and involving God, your life will fall short and become less fulfilled in your inner well-being. To gain a fulfilled life, learn to expand your capacity for love by expanding your consciousness.

MAKING SPIRITUAL GROWTH AN ACTIVE PART OF YOUR LIFE

With spiritual growth comes an expanded capacity for higher love. To make it an active part of your reality, it has to be integrated into your daily actions as much as possible. In other words, as you infuse your life with loving actions, you become a walking, expanding force of love. You gain confidence and courage and approach life with a loving attitude. Learn to stop blaming others for your failures but look to yourself as the author of your own circumstances. In other words, you take responsibility for your actions and the conditions that arise from them.

Chapter 3

VIEWING LIFE THROUGH THE EYES OF LOVE

THROUGH THE EYES OF LOVE

Through the eyes of love, your life will positively impact others.

Through the eyes of love, you will see the beauty in all life.

Through the eyes of love, you will be less judgmental.

Through the eyes of love, you will see more clearly the Divine Spirit in action in your life as well as the lives of others.

Through the eyes of love, the Divine Spirit will pull away the curtain of illusion, and the truth will lay bare before you, and you will see the truth for what it is.

Through the eyes of love, you will bring out the best in others.

Through the eyes of love, you will be more forgiving.

Through the eyes of love, you will be more compassionate.

VIEWING LIFE FROM A HIGHER PERSPECTIVE

Leaning on the Divine Spirit helps one view life from a higher perspective, above worry, personal bias, and fear. Such conditions will facilitate bringing higher love into the foreground. In that state, free of interference from the mind's constraints, awakened to higher love, and with a clear, expansive view, you will realize love is the essence of all life.

SOMETHING GREATER THAN ONESELF

All positive life missions are rooted in love, whether evident to the outer eye or not. Life missions with a transformative impact tend to have the same underlying source—love for something greater than oneself and a love for improving conditions. They aim at some goal of a higher nature for the good of humankind. It behooves one to be one of the few who strive to rise to greater heights—to something greater than oneself—to help humankind move forward.

LIVING WITH LOVE

With love, life becomes more abundant and fulfilling.

With love, no room is left for fear.

With love, you can do the impossible.

With love, you will touch others at a deeper level

With love, you will serve life selflessly

With love, you have the key to life

With love, you will walk this earth on holly ground

VIEWING LIFE MORE CLEARLY

Approaching higher truth with neutrality and purity of heart enables one to view things more closely and, therefore, more clearly, like a telescope that helps bring something out of our reach closer for a clearer view. When the lens of the telescope, your inner eye, is clouded and tarnished, it loses its ability to see with clarity, and one is bound to see a partial image—partial truth. Remove the clouding, and the truth shall shine through with greater clarity. So look to the inner self with a neutral attitude through a clear lens, and you will see and receive the truth fully and in greater measure. Divine love shall be your reward.

LISTENING TO YOUR HEART

Practice listening to your heart regularly. Let this be your way to receive guidance about serving life and helping others, and with that, you will practically become a messenger of love. Listening with your spiritual ears allows you to open your heart to God's presence, infusing you with love. Living your life from that vantage point, you will become a living, expanding love magnet.

GAINING INNER WEALTH

To gain inner wealth, you must surrender all to God without unduly holding onto anything material and psychic. This does not mean you can't have material possessions. You can have all the material things you want as long as they do not possess you. Instead, develop a healthy attitude toward them so they don't rule you. You need to be in a position where you would still maintain your equilibrium if you were to lose them. Remember that letting go might create a fear of losing one's possessions. It helps to remember that by losing anything material with no real value, we gain something invaluable: priceless inner wealth. In a state of detachment, we gain favor from God—spiritual wealth, such as joy, wisdom, and spiritual freedom—and we awaken to the light within us, which begins to shine ever so brightly. With God's light awakened in us, the clutter obstructing our vision clears, and we bask in the presence of divine love. We then discover there's no greater wealth than inner spiritual wealth, which is love for God and His creations.

OBSTACLES AS STEPPING STONES

As long as we live, we will go through experiences that may sometimes make us stumble and fall. Each time we fall, it is because we violated a spiritual law known or unknown to us. We failed to recognize a lesson embedded in that obstacle. It helps to remember that an obstacle is a stepping stone that Soul is supposed to climb over to ascend to the next level in realizing who and what It is as a loving spark of God. As we get back up from the fall, we awaken to the latent splendor of love within ourselves. It helps to be mindful that if we have love as an active part of our daily life, we always have God's presence. Love is the key ingredient that elevates our lives as we overcome obstacles that are placed on our path. Ever ascending to new heights and an increased love capacity.

GRATITUDE

Without gratitude for God's blessings in our lives, no matter how rich in material things or finances we are, there will always be a lack of fulfillment, and a feeling of inadequacy will prevail. Love sustains you and gives you a sense of well-being like no other feeling. When you love another in that unique, sincere, open-hearted way, your heart expands and fills with gratitude for the gift of life. Gratitude opens your heart so that only your heart can understand, which the mind cannot grasp. With heartfelt gratitude and understanding, the mind can then play its rightful role as an instrument for Soul, executing Soul's love wishes designed to expand and enhance your life - inner and outer. And as you approach life with a grateful heart, your heart center naturally fills with love.

SEEING THINGS WITH DEEPER UNDERSTANDING

As you keep moving forward and learning from your mistakes, you will find life and your experiences become more rewarding, and your life, in turn, becomes more joyful. That does not mean there may not be pain, losses, or grief in your life. The difference lies in the fact that your capacity to understand the harsh realities of life expands. The expanded understanding enables you to see things a little more clearly—therefore, you become more responsible for your actions, less judgmental, less critical, more compassionate, and more loving.

TRANSCENDING THE MIND

God supports all life by His very presence in all living forms. Seeing, recognizing, and acknowledging God's presence in living things expands and improves one's relationship with all life, bringing joy, freedom, love, and depth of awareness beyond the grasp of the mind. By transcending the mind in order to use the inner eyes of Soul, we will begin to see, recognize, embrace, and live the essentials of God rooted in God's love for all life.

BEAUTY IN ALL

Beauty is an inseparable part of the essence of God found in all life. This implies that all forms of life, in whatever shape, size, condition, or configuration, have love and beauty as their inner makeup.

How can all have beauty in them, including snakes, roaches, and mosquitos? You might wonder. All these creatures have beauty because God is always at the core of all living things. Since they have an aspect of God as an essential ingredient, they all have God's beauty in them, whether you see it or not. As our vision gets more acute, we can see more beauty in all life. The more we expand our consciousness, the clearer our sight, and the clearer we can see God's beauty in life. We can only see in life what we realize within ourselves. The higher we go, the further and better we can see, and the more of God's beauty we can recognize and appreciate. God is beautiful—period! Therefore, all God's creatures have beauty in them.

RELATIVITY OF BEAUTY

Beauty is relative at a superficial level. What might be beautiful to you might not appear the same to another person. So, judge not and do not impose your idea of beauty on others. Unless you walk in their shoes, view things through their lens, and feel love in their way, you won't know what makes the person find something or someone beautiful. From the human perspective, that is the relativity of beauty.

THE HIDDEN BEAUTY

Whether or not you see beauty in someone or something, all things have beauty in them, which is God's beauty because He, our maker, is beautiful. Therefore, all living forms fashioned from God's cloth have a seed of beauty and divine love embedded in them. Your task is to awaken to this beauty and divine love latent within you. Once awakened, you can see beyond the illusion of the artificial layers hiding your inner, glowing beauty. The hidden beauty is only seen by one who has a sincere heart and whose eyes are open enough to view the hidden beauty and embrace it in fullness.

VIEWING LIFE FROM A HIGHER PERSPECTIVE

Without love, the difficulties of the day can become unmanageable. Stress can get the better of you. To live a more balanced life in which challenges of the day don't throw you off balance, learn to step back and view things through the eyes of love. Genuinely ask yourself what love would do if you were in such a challenging situation. You may find that through the eyes of love, you will see things from a higher perspective and become more tolerant of others' mistakes, attitudes, shortcomings, and your own.

FACING CHALLENGES

With a loving, positive attitude, you will handle challenging situations and obstacles with less worry, less fear, and more patience in a relaxed state. Thus, remaining connected to the Divine Spirit as your daily partner in all situations. In this relaxed state, your inner creative channels will remain open, keeping you connected to God's love, guidance, and protection. This allows you to face challenges with confidence and with a level head. From this vantage point, you will see things with the eyes of Soul and have a clearer vision. Through the eyes of Soul, you can see more clearly, enabling you to face challenges confidently and positively.

POSITIVE CHANGES

Where there is harmony and peace among people, the element that renders situations peaceful is love. Love also brings about positive changes so life can move in its natural order, in love's time, ever so slowly forward (even though it may not appear so amid unpleasant events). Remember that sometimes positive changes can be preceded by breaking down old ways and outmoded patterns. This can happen through wars, calamities, or natural disasters designed to pave a new way. As the apparent disorder settles, a new order emerges, and we rarely return to the old, antiquated ways. Adaptations are instituted, and life moves on, forward or backward, depending on the type of change, for change does not always mean progress, even though all progress requires change.

THE REAL YOU

In you, the physical temple exists the real you called Soul. It is Soul that is equipped with the faculties to love self, others, and God. Through the senses of Soul, you can directly commune with the Divine Spirit. This real you, Soul, is an independent entity that exists independent of the mind and its passions. Soul is what enables you to make a loving connection with life and God. You as Soul never dies, It is always a happy entity, thus realizing yourself as Soul, awakens your inner happy nature which will result in a feeling of contentment and self-reliance. It behooves you to learn to go within and learn more about your true self—a loving, happy, inner Soul Self. The more you learn about yourself as Soul, the more you know yourself and the more joyful you will become.

YOUR LESSONS ARE NOT OTHERS' LESSONS

You ought to be patient, compassionate, and loving when someone else's lesson seems insignificant, for their journey is not yours, and their values may not be yours. What might appear easy for you might be difficult for them, and vice versa. This is the reality of life and our unique journeys. Each person has a quest in life, which comes with its own lessons. Though these lessons vary, they have one common denominator: to learn to see and discover love in all things ultimately. We will then fulfill our destiny—our journey to the divine home of pure love.

THE BLESSING OF LOVE BEHIND EVERY FOLD

Love is hidden behind every negative or positive façade, awaiting its discovery. Hence, there's the blessing of love behind every unpleasant event, adversity, or loss. The challenge is seeing the hidden blessing and making it an active and helpful part of your life. Understanding the love lesson behind every wrinkle and fold will enable you to unfold and thus understand why things are the way they are. With a better understanding, you can move a little more smoothly through life.

THE GIFT OF BEAUTY

The more beauty you see in life, the more loving you become. With that, you become a more loving Soul who embraces life, knowing all life has beauty even though, at times, it might not appear so. There's beauty everywhere to the one whose heart and spiritual eyes are open. Love becomes a daily experience. This brings joy and gratitude for God's gift of beauty in all animated and inanimate forms, for they all reflect God's innate grace and wonder hidden in them.

THE VOICE OF LOVE

The voice of love is in every aspect of life. Every sound you hear has a voice of love in it, for it's a voice of God in action, and it is what renders all of God's creations alive. All life is centered and anchored in love as its basis for existence, no matter how negative it may appear to the human eye. Trust that all things have love in them and speak the voice of love from the inner recesses of their being. The audible and inaudible voice of love is what allows communication, verbal or nonverbal, possible among living forms.

TUNING IN

Learning to tune in to God's essence will open your spiritual eyes. With these, you can see God's action, so you might begin to recognize Its manifestation in your daily life, often in a subtle manner. You will start to pick up on its activity through words spoken by others and through deeds done with love in which the hand of God is in operation. This is so because your heart is rendered purer, and with a pure heart filled with God's love, you can see life around you through the eyes of love.

THE BEAUTY OF LOVE

Most of us pay the barest attention to what love says. It's about time we started to pay a little more attention to becoming happier and more loving individuals. Love must always be at the center of our actions, plans, and goals. When love is regularly infused in what we do, it transforms you into a better and more loving person with higher ethics. With love as a primary motivation in your actions, you will stay connected to the ever-loving presence of God. With this strong connection, the beauty of love will grace your life in a profound, organic way.

LETTING LOVE PERMEATE YOUR ACTIONS

When you let love permeate what you do, your life starts to change for the better. Things you wish to have that add value to your life may gravitate toward you. Challenging things necessary for your experience may become easier to handle. Difficult things may become easier to resolve. Complicated things may become less complex as you view life through the lens of your higher, inner self. Things may take a new turn because you have intentionally injected love into all you do. Soul, which is your true self and the highest viewpoint within all of us, has God-given faculties that can enable you to see new occurrences in life most clearly. However, remember that these creative faculties may lie dormant if not awakened and engaged. You can awaken these latent faculties through prayer, meditation, contemplation, or chanting HU, an ancient love song to God.

Chapter 4

LOVE IN
ACTION

ACTIONS MOTIVATED BY LOVE

Any action motivated by and done with love has the power to open the hearts of those involved. Therefore, the benefactor and the recipient benefit in a like manner even though the outer experience might not appear the same. However, the inner core of their mutual interaction may have a cohesive effect, which may strengthen their relationship. Hence, it behooves one to choose and engage in acts driven by a greater love for someone or something positive, which creates an outflow for more love. Engaging in actions motivated by love is always positive as long as love is shared unconditionally.

MAKING LOVE AN ACTIVE PART OF YOUR LIFE

How do you make love an active part of your life? You can start by disciplining yourself according to love's ways. Focus on God and ask what God would do when you face a situation in which you are called to serve another in need of your help. This approach can open the door within you to let God partake in your actions. This would yield a more positive outcome than leaving it all to your limited human effort and strength. Whenever you include God in your actions, a desirable outcome ensues in one way or another, in God's time and on His terms. You will not always be aware of such blessings, but sometimes you may notice a spontaneous improvement in your life in one way or another. That's love enhancing your life.

A BETTER WAY TO NAVIGATE THROUGH LIFE

Many people go through life blindly, without considering that once God is allowed to lead us, He can show us a better way to navigate life. So look to God and seek guidance so He can show you the way to a better life, which can yield the utmost fulfillment and make your life a little more joyful and filled with more love despite the difficulties you may encounter. With God's guidance, difficulties will become opportunities for spiritual growth, which is why they are there—stepping stones to successively better conditions in your life.

MOVING ALONG IN LIFE

To move along smoothly in life, we must learn to step back, stay calm, reflect, and recognize that every negative situation is there to teach us something positive about life. It's a blessing in disguise. A gold mine of wisdom, love, and new learning is embedded in it. With the lesson learned, we move along with an increased capacity for humility, understanding, and love.

INNER PEACE

A wise person always seeks inner peace as one knows no real peace exists in the outer world; hence, he looks within. It takes total trust in the higher power to discipline oneself to look within to seek and embrace inner peace. One ought to have faith in God's guidance, lean upon this higher power as much as is practical, and learn to stay anchored in God's love. Once grounded from within, nothing shall shake one who dwells in God. One can watch life's drama with detachment and clear understanding, seeing life in its true light from a higher, relaxed vantage point.

OBSTACLES AS STEPPING STONES

When love is allowed to flow freely, it touches those for whom it is intended and bestows upon them all things positive because love uplifts. It opens people's hearts. It nourishes those who are receptive to it. It lifts and honors them. It has the power to heal a broken heart. Love can only freely flow when obstacles are viewed as stepping stones to higher love. As you surrender to the experience of love, love will infuse you with a profound sense of well-being within your inner core.

ACTS OF LOVE

If you can do something to meet someone's particular need, then that act has love. If you can do a deed without the need to make yourself look better, more knowledgeable, or smarter than another, then that deed will become a carrier of love. Any act that lifts another to a better version of themselves, even a little bit, is of love. The act can take any form, such as giving your time, money, or positive thoughts toward another. Such selfless gestures are what connect Souls because they are acts of love.

INFUSING LOVE IN YOUR ACTIONS

If you make love an integral part of your daily life, your life will become dynamic and a joy to live. Infusing love into your actions daily will reflect the love you feel in your heart. Acts of this nature, so in tune with the law of love, will bring joy and love to those you give unconditional love. With love allowed to be an active part of your life, it is rendered dynamic and ever-expanding.

THINGS GET BETTER WITH LOVE

One feature of love in action in your daily life is that things get better or easier in one way or another. Things move from one lower state progressively to a more fine-tuned, higher state because love uplifts and places one on a higher level within one's inner self. Living life from this higher place can help bring more joy into your life and other people's lives within your orbit of experience. With the elevation in your experience of love, you will become more tolerant, empathetic, and forgiving of yourself and others. Passions of the mind, such as anger and undue attachment to material things that may sway your life, will have less control over you, resulting in an increased feeling of freedom. As a result, your life will get better in many respects.

YOUR UNIQUE JOURNEY

The Divine Spirit, the inner God force, called by different names in different paths, is of practical reality to those who have enough awareness, courage, and humility to follow it. How can you follow it? You can start by believing that the Divine Spirit exists even though you can't see it directly with the human eye. This will begin to steer you toward your unique journey home to God.

In time you will discover that it is by immersing yourself in love that you eventually become driven by love in all you do. It behooves you to follow the guidance of the Divine Spirit for it will lead you to experience greater love. Thus, fulfilling your mission on earth. That mission is to make God a reality in your life—not something you just talk about, but something you live to its fullest extent as much as you can.

ALLOWING GOD'S LOVE IN YOUR LIFE

Only good can come out of what you do when you let God's love into your life. Your life will run more smoothly than if you didn't allow God to work through you. If you let God operate through you, you will live by the code of love—God's love. So look to God for all you do. But don't just sit back. Make plans and set goals, but before you act on them, hand them over to God for review, fine-tuning, and upgrading. You can't go wrong if you let the Divine Spirit work with you to improve your lot. Your loving actions will sow the seeds of love and help yield better fruit.

FOLLOWING YOUR HEART'S PROMPTINGS

The truthfulness of your actions and the love you feel should guide your loving actions. With such an approach, you will find love is here for everyone if you learn how to follow your heart's promptings and pluck up enough courage to share it where needed. However, following the heart's prodding is not always easy. It takes faith and trust in the unseen, for often, what is required at the moment may contradict what logic dictates.

THE BEST COURSE OF ACTION

Just because something is true doesn't always mean you have to act on it if doing so is unnecessary and unkind. In some cases, you can either be direct or indirect. Sometimes, if you are too direct when an indirect approach best serves a situation, you could hurt another unnecessarily, and then love is lost. If something calls for immediate action, by all means, go ahead and do it directly. If leaving things alone is the best course of action to express love, then it's better to be discreet and leave it alone; it's better to be discreet and leave it alone and bless it. It will sooner or later run its natural course. Thus, the best approach is living in the moment, recognizing love at that moment, and taking the appropriate action needed to express it in alignment with love's rhythm. The best course of action is the one that is in sync with love's time in the final analysis.

A LIFE OF FULFILLMENT

Why is love the essence of all life? It is so because all life exists due to love. The Divine Spirit, God's love in action, sustains all that exists. All that has life is somehow supported and rendered alive by love. Without love, our lives will lose meaning and purpose and amount to nothing. Love expressed unconditionally for someone or something can lead to a life of fulfillment. There's no other force that has the power to bring ultimate satisfaction than love in its pure, unconditional, higher form.

LIVING ONE'S LIFE WITH INTEGRITY

Love has the power to impact your life positively. From love comes truth and a desire to live a life of integrity. Without integrity, love is undermined, and your moral compass is compromised. Learn to be a person of your word. Walk the walk. Live by the code of truth. Truth will always protect you in the end; if not now, then later. Living a life of truth is living a life close to God, for truth is the language of God. With truth as the guiding principle in all you do, you will live a life of integrity.

ACTIONS DRIVEN BY LOVE

Love always uplifts and improves anything it touches, changes, and sustains. Hence, listen to your heart to understand better which acts are driven by love and which are not. Those driven by love often, if not always, tend to open people's hearts. Actions that are not directed by love tend to close hearts. Therefore, it makes sense that we should engage in actions driven by love to find the right direction in our lives.

ACTING WITH LOVE

There's no greater love than serving a fellow human in need. Give yourself to others so love can flow from you to others and naturally back to you. Love without action to convey it is purely academic. Learn to act with love so your efforts can bear good fruit, adding value to your life. Your life will become a joy to live despite the usual challenges that are often blessings in disguise, to the extent that they compel us to grow and mature and teach us vital lessons of love, humility, and compassion.

HANDLING NEGATIVE KARMA

One way of handling the negative cycle caused by our past bad karma is to hand it over and let God take over whatever unpleasant circumstance you find yourself in. Surrendering to God helps you let go of a negative situation, whereupon you become less worried, less fearful, less anxious, less tense, and more relaxed because you know it is safe in God's hands. Trust in God is essential; otherwise, surrender would be merely a mental concept without practical significance. True surrender works best in an environment of faith in the higher power. Implicit trust in the higher power can make you relax. It becomes easier to let go of your excessive hold on the unpleasant situation when relaxed. In this state, you allow God to take over to have His greatest impact in whatever way He sees fit and act according to His Will. And whatever the outcome, rest assured it is always to your benefit even though it might sometimes not appear so at first glance. By letting go of your tight hold on your negative situation in such a way, you invite God to have an active role in your daily affairs. Who better to seek help to rearrange our bad karmic account than the always merciful, all-powerful God?

UNIVERSALITY OF LOVE

Love is essential for human survival and development. Without love, your life will diminish in value and depth. This is because love is the Divine Spirit which sustains and nourishes all life. This divine love, by nature, is a purer and higher form of love than human love that demands conditions. Universal love also subsumes human love, making our relationships and reconnection with God possible. Being universal, it undergirds all life and touches all hearts irrespective of religion or lack thereof, regardless of whether you are evil or good. All life has love at its epicenter; the continuity of life depends on it. That is the all-encompassing, uplifting nature and power of the universality of love. It's God's essence in action!

LISTENING TO THE INNER SUBTLE VOICE OF GOD

Learn to love others the right way so positive results come out of any situation with the potential for love to flourish. You can do so by tuning in to the moment's needs, listening to your heart, and following your heart's promptings so your actions align with your heart's guidance. Love will flow more abundantly with proper judgment and execution of requisite action. Love yourself, love others, love life, love God, love all, but be wise about sharing your love with others. More importantly, follow your heart; a subtle inner voice of God uniquely speaks through your heart to prompt and guide you in the right direction. Practice listening to that subtle inner voice whispered by God to your heart.

CARRIERS OF LOVE

Without love, nothing moves toward growth, advancement, and improvement in the true, uplifting sense. Everything that grows and gets better does so because love is the undercurrent. Though love is invisible to the human eye, it manifests in actions that carry love, such as gratitude, forgiveness, and compassion. Your subsequent actions will convey the message of love according to the core principles you uphold that govern your actions.

LOVE CATALYSTS

Any action that acts as a catalyst for love has the potential to evoke love in others. When this love is shared, it creates an inner condition instantaneously in which more love from God fills your heart. With this, your heart expands as it triggers an inflow from the higher source—God—and you pass it on to others through your selfless actions. Such is how love issues from God are passed on to you so you may share it with those whose hearts are open and receptive to love. Any act that accelerates the outflow of love is a catalyst for love. Such could happen through a creative process, such as a talent or hobby, someone you love, God you pray to, work you do that you love, or any action that opens your heart and others' hearts.

CONNECTING WITH OTHERS

Without love, your spiritual journey will become a stalemate, and your spiritual sight will fail. One's journey gets hampered by obstacles placed in one's path as one's sight dims, rendering one incapable of having a clear view of where one heads in life. Thus, life gets impeded in one way or another because of your diminished ability to see life's blessings and guidance, resulting in a decreased ability to share love when needed. It helps to remember that sharing love with others creates a love outflow, enabling you to connect with others at a deeper level. With that, you become more spiritual. This connection goes beyond your circle of friends; it extends to your inner guide, guardian angel, higher power, or God within. Through love, you are guided in the right direction in pivotal moments and thus steered progressively toward God. So, to stay spiritually active, learn to share love, for in doing so, you connect with others.

LIGHTING UP THE ROAD AHEAD

Placing your attention on God via daily rededication can open your window to Soul, allowing more light to illuminate your road ahead, laying bare unsuspecting traps hidden on your path. When your inner light illuminates the road ahead, you can see what danger lurks behind the illusion of life with better clarity. With that, you can meet what is coming in a more prepared manner and have a better chance to overcome, avoid, or surmount obstacles in your life.

ALLOWING MORE LOVE TO FLOW]

Always tune in to the needs of the moment. Listen to and follow your heart so your actions will be in sync with the needs of the moment and more love can flow more freely. Love yourself, love others, love life, love God, but be wise about giving your love to others. If not, the world will teach you that there's a cost to indiscriminate, thoughtless giving of love, as it requires action on your part in one way or another.

DEALING WITH NEGATIVE SITUATIONS

One way to avoid creating negative situations for ourselves is by blessing the situation, no matter how painful. By doing so, we are not feeding the problem negative energy that can compound it but instead allowing the negative energy to dry out and run its natural course sooner rather than later, thus sparing us unnecessary pain. With the resolution of a negative situation, we rise, ascend to a new place within our inner being, and hence experience more love.

RESPONDING TO CHALLENGES

Life challenges are part of the cosmic plan and, thus, will always be a part of our lives. They are there for our benefit, to polish us and make us better, wiser, stronger, loving, and compassionate. How you respond to challenges can make a difference in how you proceed. Rush, get into knee-jerk reaction mode, and you are liable to stumble and fall. Thus, it behooves you to learn to step back for a better view and avoid an impulsive reaction when you unexpectedly face a challenging situation. With a better view, you can make better decisions about surmounting challenges or counteract them instead of reacting to them. Reacting can blind you to the true light of the situation, thus missing the lesson embedded in the challenge.

MAKING LIFE A JOY TO LIVE

With increased gratitude for the gift of life, you reach higher heights of fulfillment. It's a blessing to live a life of love, drenched in love, for it makes your life a joy. With love like this, your life has meaning and depth beyond measure. Living a life of love enables you to live following God's will to the best of your ability and level of acceptance. Thus, you live in obedience to God and experience bliss beyond this earthly experience. Therefore, by living in alignment with the law of love, your life becomes joyful for the most part.

A PRACTICAL REALITY

As you live in alignment with God's will, you realize love is the essence of life. This makes you appreciate that life is a gift of love from God. To live this love and make it a practical reality, you must integrate it into your daily life. For love to be real to you, it has to be practical. It is what makes your life authentic. Without love, a feeling of inadequacy will always prevail. The remedy for this inadequacy is finding a way to manifest, share, and express love somehow. It could be done in innumerable ways, such as loving a fellow human, adopting a pet, taking up a hobby, helping in need, and any other ways in which actions are done with honesty without the need for repayment, recognition, or praise.

Chapter 5

THE HIGHEST LOVE

OPENING THE DOOR TO GOD'S LOVE, THE HIGHEST LOVE WITHIN

How do you open the door to God's love, the highest love within, wherein the answers to life exist? One way is through honest efforts to cultivate the latent love within through prayer, meditation, or chanting HU. HU is a love song to God that does not belong to any religion or path. Chanting helps expand one's consciousness, brings inner peace, and opens one's heart to divine love. Love thus cultivated will grow in proportion to what you are willing to accept, embrace, and give back to life. In the process, your consciousness will begin to expand. In turn, your ability to understand and recognize God's love all around us naturally increases. With love as a new guiding force in your life, your life is transformed and becomes more fulfilling.

YOUR HEART'S PROMPTINGS

Follow your heart's promptings. By following your heart's silent whispers, you will discover that therein lies God's love, His gentle voice, the inner compass to guide you to more love hidden in various facades awaiting your awakening to them through the purification of your heart. It takes courage to follow God's inner promptings, for God's ways are not always our limited human ways. God is always trying to lift us and take us a step beyond where we are now so we can grow and become more mature, awakened, loving Souls.

EXPERIENCING LOVE

The more you look to the inner self for pure love, the more of it you will cultivate, garner, and experience. Yet having it in your heart shouldn't be the be-all and end-all. You must go beyond feeling and apply it daily to manifest it as a practical reality. You must create an outflow of it to the world and, in its application, yield the abundant fruit of more love. This will enable you to experience more love in your day-to-day life as you increase your ability to share more love with others.

HEARING GOD'S LOVING GUIDANCE

When you hear God's guiding, gentle voice within the depths of your heart, take comfort in knowing He bestows you blessings of joy, love, and inner tranquility. Honor this experience, seize it, embrace it, and heed it. It's God's way of guiding your life in the right direction. It may not be easy to follow, but rest assured that being God's way will be the right direction. So fear not.

LIVING A LIFE OF LOVE

With love, you realign with your real mission on Earth: to learn how to love genuinely and deeply to add value and meaning to your life. By loving truly, you are living a life guided by the Divine Spirit, in which the invisible hand of God protects you and uplifts you as you obey Its edicts.

FERTILE BREEDING GROUND FOR GOD'S LOVE

Look always to keep your consciousness clean and pure. The purity of thought and deed makes for a fertile breeding ground for God's love. In this fertile state, God's love is reflected, and those open to it will feel it, bask in it, and be lifted by it. Keep in mind that fertile grounds come in different guises. A difficult time can be fertile ground; therefore, it is a blessing in disguise, an opportunity to grow spiritually, depending on how you respond. Approach it with a positive attitude, steadfastly, without complaining or assigning blame for the condition, and you will eventually overcome it. Thus, grow spiritually in your consciousness, in your capacity for more love,

LETTING GOD GUIDE YOU

God may bring something you didn't ask for into your life because that's what you may have needed to enable you to get to the next level in your journey. So, asking for guidance and leaving it in God's hands can help guide you to the best course of action. Leave it to God to guide you on the next step, even if you think you know what you need to do. Such an attitude of letting God guide you despite making plans to take a specific course of action allows God to have a hand in your plans. God's plan is always higher and better than your limited personal plan. Adjusting and aligning your plan to God's plan is one way to fulfill His dream for you.

LOVE IN ITS PURE FORM

In pure love, answers to all the questions are revealed because love in its higher form denotes the presence of God. In God exists all man's heavenly desires, all possibilities in which one's answers, answers for asked questions, unasked ones, unknown questions, and unanswered questions exist. This is so because it is only in the higher state in which you find corresponding pure love that you find the light of God, which illuminates your inner sight. Hence, you become more insightful, more perspective, and far-seeing beyond the limits of human consciousness. In that higher state, you can have an expanded view of higher reality, bringing aspects of truth beyond human consciousness's reach into view.

PARTAKING OF GOD'S LOVE

How do you partake of God's love? You can talk about God's love all you want, but talking alone doesn't bring you closer to God. It's in your actions that you partake of God's love. What actions can enable you to actively partake of God's love? Simply put, it's the actions that involve serving another unselfishly, such as sacrificing for another in need, lifting another, bringing healing to another, and opening others' hearts. Such actions help free Soul from the bindings of this material world. Once you are free from the constraints of this material world, you experience increased joy, and your heart becomes filled with love. From this vantage point, you can naturally serve others unconditionally and help others reconnect with God. It's such actions that will help you partake of God's love.

HIGHER TRUTH

Higher truth always uplifts. However, it is sometimes not easy to decipher and accept. Reading books does not guarantee acquiring truth, but rather, head knowledge. Watching others go through their personal experiences does not necessarily mean you fully understand the heart of their experience. By going through the experience, you know the nature of the truth as it relates to you. Through the right experiences that enable you to gain higher truth, you awaken to higher love, which you can, in turn, share with others if done appropriately—unconditionally.

LOVE-BRINGING MORE FULFILLMENT TO YOUR LIFE

Seek, accept, and share love to bring more fulfillment to your life. It's a natural human and spiritual need and impulse to maximize your experience of love in whatever form and in whatever way fits you. Behind all love is God's presence, often expressed according to each individual's capacity and ability. Your life will be filled with love if love becomes the basis and compass for your actions.

THE GIFT OF LOVE

Through direct experience, you will realize that the love you seek is right here near you. To find it, keep your heart open. With an open heart, the invisible force of love will lead you to go to places where you will find it, meet you halfway, or seek you out and find you right where it is supposed to find you. When the gift of love comes about, have the courage and humility to accept it, seize it naturally and creatively, and make it an active part of your life so it can add value to your life.

UNDERSTANDING GOD

You can only understand God in proportion to the degree to which you have expanded your consciousness, which is your capacity to accept God's love. Once you do, you realize that God should always be the pillar you lean on, consciously or unconsciously, as you go through life and its challenges. Remember that you better understand God through using your spiritual faculties since God is in spirit form or formless. It just makes sense that you employ your spiritual faculties to make direct contact with the spirit of God to begin to gain a modicum of understanding of who and what God is in the spiritual sense. This understanding can bring about a transformation and enable you to experience God's love. Anchored in God's love, your subsequent actions should follow high ethical standards.

EMBRACING GOD'S LOVE

God's love, which naturally emanates from God, should be the force we need to embrace and accept wholeheartedly, for It affords those ready love, freedom, and joy. If God, the source of love, can bring these positive qualities, it is wise to love God above everything else, for everything else depends on Him, whether one is aware or not. Nothing exists that has no dependence on God, consciously or unconsciously, for survival and spiritual nourishment. So learn to embrace God within, or whichever divine being or higher power you seek for your spiritual guidance and succor.

EXPRESSION OF THE LOVE OF GOD THROUGH WORK

The love of God comes through when you pay close attention to details and fulfill what you need to do to bring about a positive change in whatever area of your endeavor. The best way to express your love for God is by engaging in acts that open people's hearts. These deeds activate the essence of God through your work that is done with perfection, which acts as a conduit for God's love. You bring God's love to bear through your work, which is done well. So, learn to do your best, and through your work, you will bring out the essence of God and, in turn, open others' hearts.

KNOWING GOD A LITTLE BETTER

With the right experiences and expanded consciousness, you come to know God a little better—His reality, His presence, and His role in your life. God is the ultimate reality of which you ought to aspire to become a conscious part. However, you cannot grasp God's limitless enormity fully. That would be tantamount to replacing God. You can only understand God in proportion to the degree to which you purify your heart and to the extent you sincerely desire God.

TRUE LOVERS OF GOD

The reality of God is only for those who love the truth, take the trouble, and make an honest effort to ascend to the highest truth within their inner being. These are the true lovers of God, for they sacrifice a lot in giving up their creature comforts, fears, egos, and undue attachments to ascend to heights beyond the earthly constraints that hold humankind in captivity.

HIDDEN LOVE

How does love manifest itself in different forms? This is a question worth pondering to gain a glimpse into the eternal essence of love. The challenge in understanding the enormity of love is that it has many manifestations that need to be recognized and understood. Love is the essence of life; all life has love at its central point, often hidden, awaiting its activation by awakened hearts that seek it sincerely and in earnest. The presence of love in all things makes all things have life. Without love, there would be no life. Thus, the more love you have and give, the more alive you become.

COOPERATING WITH THE DIVINE SPIRIT

Strive to cultivate divine love and learn to cooperate with Its impeccable guidance. It is in your cooperation that it cooperates with you. This reciprocal relationship creates a bond that enables you and other Souls to be in loving service to one another. So wake up and recognize and appreciate the love of God that is here and now. It is here for the taking if you can follow Its guidance and fulfill the conditions needed to make direct contact with It.

AN EASIER WAY TO HEAR THE INNER VOICE OF GOD

You can hear the inner voice of God only when your heart is relaxed, ready, and open to God's love. In that calm, unbiased, neutral state, you can gradually begin to hear God's voice with your inner ears. It can come in many forms, such as a nonverbal voice, direct knowingness without recourse to the mind, a nudge, a sign, and any number of ways unique to you as an individual based on your level of acceptance. Hearing God's gentle inner voice is a blessing, for it comes to lift you and grace you with God's love.

STAYING OPEN TO THE LOVE OF GOD

How do you stay open to the love of God? It might sound easy, but it is more complex than it seems. If it were easy, everyone would remain open to God's love. It is difficult because God comes in simple ways that people usually don't understand and, therefore, overlook. Living in this world dominated by materiality doesn't make it easier to open oneself to God. If you were to assume a position of neutrality, you would find yourself opening up to the love of God. Spiritual growth is essential if we aspire to improve our relationship with life and God, which can bring more joy into our lives. It takes an opening of our hearts, sidestepping the ego, and surrendering into the hands of God to stay open to the love of God.

UNDERSTANDING LOVE

To delve deeper into what love is, you ought to learn to step back for a better view of the play of life as it unfolds before you. It's one way to live consciously with care, love, and respect for life. Such a measured, deliberate approach and examination of life activity can help you understand what love truly is in its subtle, covert, and overt manifestations. Keeping your heart open and delving deeper into the source of love, God can deepen your understanding of love in its pure, divine form.

RECOGNIZING LOVE IN ITS VARIED FORMS

Failing to recognize love can make a person fall short of its optimal fulfillment. It behooves you to awaken your heart so that in the awakened state, the higher spiritual state, you can recognize love in its many forms, which will, in turn, enrich your life in many ways. The question becomes, how do you recognize love in its many forms? It is through your heart that you will recognize love in any form. A heart that is pure, receptive, and giving can recognize love in its many varied forms.

THE EXPERIENCE OF LOVE

Love defies logic because it is felt with the heart, not the mind. Only the heart can understand it, not reason born out of the mind. The mind has only a logical, narrow understanding of love, which limits your understanding of love as an element that issues from God's eternity. If you want to immerse yourself in the profound richness of love, let go of the overly logical part of yourself and learn to love from the vantage point of your heart.

LOVE ROOTED IN THE DIVINE ESSENCE

Once you cultivate love in your heart, it yields feelings of peace, joy, and self-assurance. These are positive feelings that enable you to appreciate life even more. Your happiness is no longer dependent on unreliable, limited external factors but instead felt within, independent of whether you have material possessions. You feel content because your love is not born of material things that never quench your desire but is rooted in the indestructible essence of God. Once rooted in something permanent, such as the divine essence, you can't help but feel assured, confident, and joyful because your well-being depends on something with permanent value: God. And in God, you walk confidently with an open heart and thus appreciate life more.

SEARCHING FOR THE LOVE OF GOD

The love of God exists everywhere, but not everyone feels it deeply. It's ubiquitous yet not accessible to everyone in its pure form. It comes in varied shapes and ways, but most people do not always recognize it. As a result, many people don't believe it's there, even when it's before their eyes. So people lament the lack of God's love, yet it is just before them in the fundamental aspects of life where they don't think to look. They look for it in high places, everywhere except where it exists, hidden in their hearts. Look there as a starting point. Listen for the whisper of love in your heart and follow your heart's promptings.

THE POWER OF HAPPINESS

If you have love as an active part of your daily life, you have God's presence daily. How do you have love in the first place? First, believe that love is the key ingredient that can make your life better—in the sense that you will have happiness in some measure to make your life worth living. Without happiness, stress will become a bane of your life. Happiness is a state of being in which Soul, a happy entity, permeates your human consciousness and thus nourishes you. Without an ounce of happiness, your life would become intolerable. A happy state is a state of balance. And by God, we need balance in our lives, although it is elusive and often hard to maintain if we rush through life. Thus, taking your time to go through life and adapt as changes inevitably come about is wise. With happiness, you will live your life with a grateful heart. With a thankful heart for the gift of life, your heart will ever be filled with Love. With a loving heart, you will hear God's music and see God's guiding light.

EXPERIENCING GOD'S LOVE

With the daily practice of seeing life from the perspective of love, you will practically experience God's love in your everyday life, and because of that, you will live life with more joy and fulfillment. It takes an open, loving attitude, total surrender to God, and implicit faith in the unseen power of God to let go of one's outer undue attachments. Once this is accomplished, it is possible to surrender into God's loving arms and experience God's love to the maximum of your capacity. Life has a way of setting up conditions in which, through challenging situations, you rise to new, untapped heights in which you touch the cloth of God. And gradually, ultimately, voilà! You claim your throne as God's awakened child experientially.

THE ENRICHING POWER OF LOVE

Your attention and focus should be on finding the purest love, embracing it, and sharing it. In making love an active part of your daily life, fear will recede, and your life will expand as love becomes integral, even though you may not always be aware of it. Hence, as love continually graces your life, and as you make it the ideal to which you aspire and strive to live, everything else will fall into place, expanding your life and making it an adventure, dynamic, and a joy to live. That is the enriching power of love if you make it the guiding principle in all you do.

About the Author

Eric Chifunda is a New York-based Occupational Therapist who works as an independent contractor, licensed in New York and New Jersey. He is also an artist who interweaves representational and visionary elements in his artwork. He strives to create art that is uplifting. You can view some of his artwork on FineArtAmerica.com.

He is also an actor who occasionally does acting.

Awarded Editors' Choice Award by the International Library of Poetry (2006)

www.ingramcontent.com/pod-product-compliance
Lightning Source LLC
Chambersburg PA
CBHW031054310726
48969CB00007B/2276